Elizabeth Cole

I Am Stronger
Than Anxiety

This book is dedicated to all my young readers.
You are my real inspiration and love!
Thank you!

This book belongs to

....

....

It was a sunny weekend – time for some fun.
Nick's dad planned a camping trip with his son.
Nick was excited to spend the day with Dad.
But then he thought of all the worries he had.

"How will I sleep without my favorite toys?
How will I sleep if the thunder makes noise?
What if I see monsters hiding in the trees?
What if I get stung by a hardworking bee?"

Nick's hands started to sweat and his mouth felt dry.
He was so upset that he could start to cry.
His whole world felt like it was turned inside out.
He was feeling anxious. There was no doubt.

During the drive to the mountains, Nick didn't talk.
Dad set up the tent while Nick went for a walk.
Still worried, Nick wandered and looked all around.
He saw a raccoon writing a note on the ground.

"Hey, there. What are you writing?" Little Nick asked.
The raccoon replied, but kept scribbling fast.
"I moved to a new den where the forest ends.
I was afraid I wouldn't make any new friends.

So, I write down my worries here on a note,
and then throw away everything that I wrote."
Nick took some paper and wrote his worries too.
He scribbled them fast until he was through.

Nick and the raccoon tossed their notes away.
"I feel so much better now, I have to say."

Nick thanked the raccoon and continued his walk. Then he heard someone singing behind a big rock. It was a moose with funny antlers on his head. "Hello. That's a beautiful song," Little Nick said.

The moose said, "I am nervous before my football game.
When I have to go to the dentist, I feel the same.

So, whenever I'm nervous, I sing this song.
It helps me feel better, it helps me feel strong."

The moose taught Nick the words and he sang along.
They walked through the woods singing this song:

"Worries, oh, worries, I will beat you all,
whether you are big, or many that are small.
I am fearless and I am brave too.
Anxiety, I am stronger than you."

Nick left the moose and saw someone new for a chat.
It was a brown bear stretching out on a mat.

The bear looked funny, wearing a toga.
"Come and join me, I'm doing yoga.
I'm trying to relax before the school play.
I'm scared and don't want my anxiety to stay."

Little Nick stood up tall next to the bear.
He took a deep breath of fresh forest air.
Together they stretched their legs and their backs.
They reached arms to the sky, then stretched their necks.

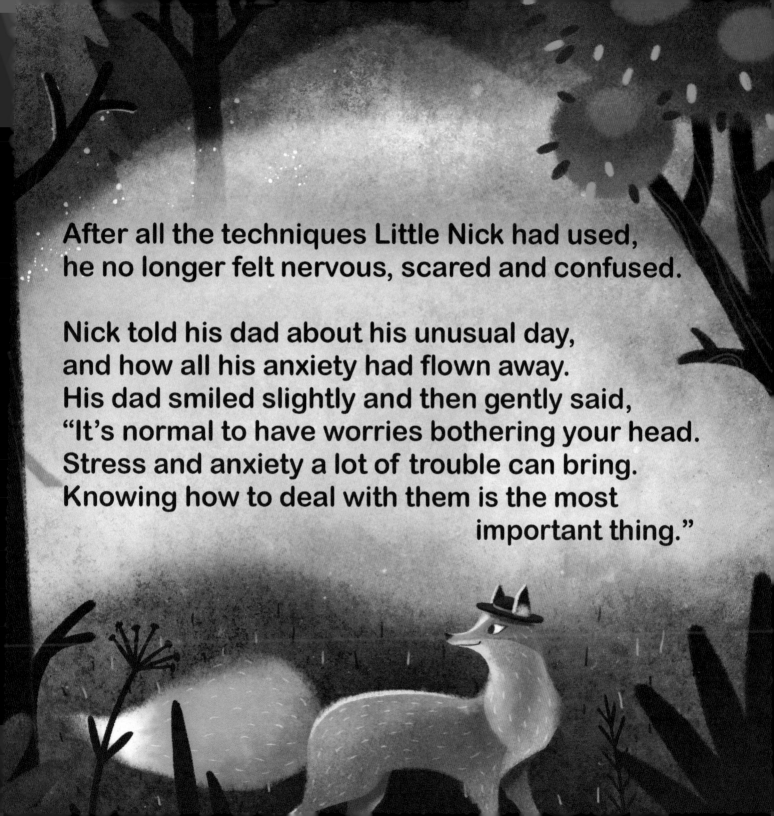

After all the techniques Little Nick had used,
he no longer felt nervous, scared and confused.

Nick told his dad about his unusual day,
and how all his anxiety had flown away.
His dad smiled slightly and then gently said,
"It's normal to have worries bothering your head.
Stress and anxiety a lot of trouble can bring.
Knowing how to deal with them is the most
important thing."

Nick was glad to share his thoughts with his dad,
and to tell him about all the worries he'd had.
The rest of their trip was relaxing and fun.
"I'm stronger than anxiety," Nick said. "And I won!"

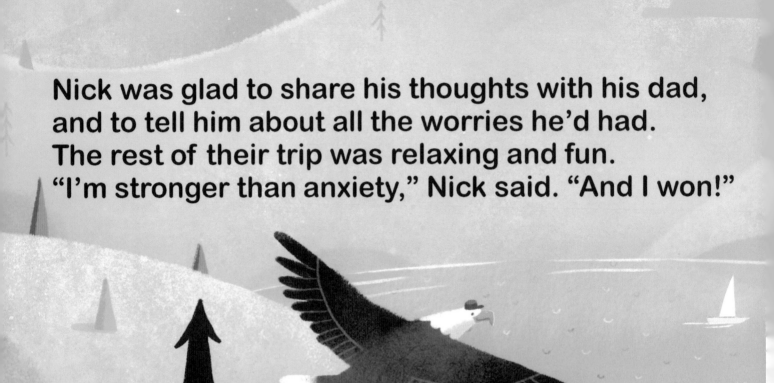

**Go here to get your
bonus calming technique for FREE!**

Dear Reader,

Thank you for purchasing my book!
This is the second story from the series "The World of Kids Emotions". The series is aimed at helping kids understand their feelings and emotions and deal with them in a funny and exciting way.

I received lots of positive comments about the first book and I hope you enjoyed this one too! Special thanks to my young readers, your feedbacks are of utmost importance and inspire me all the time!

I am very much motivated to continue Nick's adventures! So, what kind of emotion would you like to see in my next book? Please, feel free to send me your all and any thoughts and ideas.

I'm so excited to hear back from you! You can write me at elizabethcole.author@gmail.com

I would also greatly appreciate it if you could review my book.

Your input means a lot to me!

With love,
Elizabeth Cole

I'm stronger than anxiety!

Printed in Great Britain
by Amazon

78625961R00018